NEW FRONTIERS
EXPLORATION IN THE 20th CENTURY

THE WORLD OF SPACE

CASS R. SANDAK

FRANKLIN WATTS
NEW YORK LONDON TORONTO SYDNEY

All photographs courtesy of NASA except for the following: The Granger Collection: p. 4 (top);
Dennis Milon: p. 4 (bottom left and right); Sovfoto: p. 6 (bottom left); UPI/Bettmann Newsphotos: p. 6
(bottom right), p. 7 (top left); Estec Photo: p. 7 (top right); Sovfoto: p. 8 (bottom left and right), p. 9
(top left, right, and bottom left); UPI/Bettmann Newsphotos p. 9 (bottom right), p. 10 (top); Sovfoto:
p. 12 (bottom left), p. 16 (bottom left and right), p. 19 (top right); UPI/Bettmann Newsphotos: p. 22
(bottom), p. 23 (top left); Sovfoto: p. 24 (top and bottom); British Aerospace: p. 25 (top right).

FOR MY FATHER

First published in the USA
by Franklin Watts Inc.
387 Park Ave., South
New York, N.Y. 10016

First published in 1989 by
Franklin Watts
12a Golden Square
London W1R 4BA

First published in Australia
by Franklin Watts
Australia
14 Mars Road
Lane Cove, NSW 2066

US ISBN: 0-531-10459-1
UK ISBN: 0 86313 530 7
Library of Congress
Catalog Card No: 87-50904

Designed by Michael Cooper

TABLE OF CONTENTS

THE REALM OF SPACE

For thousands of years earthbound observers have looked up at the heavens and dreamed of traveling into space. In the 20th century this dream has come true. The record of what has been accomplished in four decades of space science is astonishing.

The work of several giants who studied the universe has enabled scientists to make space exploration a reality. The Polish astronomer Copernicus (1473-1543) was the first to explain how the planets move around the Sun. Galileo Galilei (1564-1642), an Italian scientist, helped make the Copernican theory better known. But his real contribution to astronomy was the invention of a telescope with lenses that magnified the view and showed details of the distant Moon and planets. Johannes Kepler (1571-1630), a German astronomer, explained how the planets and other objects move in space. And the great English mathematician, Isaac Newton (1642-1727), uncovered the laws of motion and gravity that keep the Solar System suspended in space.

Telescopes have come a long way since they were first invented, but they still rely on lenses to gather additional light and magnify, allowing us to see more. It was a telescope that allowed the discovery of the final planet in the Solar System. On February 18, 1930 Clyde Tombaugh discovered Pluto while studying photographs from the telescope at the Lowell Observatory in Flagstaff, Arizona, where he was a technician. Pluto was the first new planet to be discovered since Neptune was first seen in the 1800s: its discovery was one of the top news stories of 1930.

Scientists have used telescopes of all kinds to gather information from outer space. The reflector of California's Mount Palomar telescope, America's largest, is 5 m (200 in) across. Among today's giant telescopes is the Soviet Union's 6-m (236-in) telescope. The Smithsonian's telescope, located in Arizona, has a 4.5-m (176-in) aperture and six primary mirrors.

Above. **The Polish astronomer Copernicus studied the Solar System.** Below. **Inside and outside McDonald Observatory at Austin, Texas. The 208.28-cm (82-in) reflecting telescope has a spectrograph.**

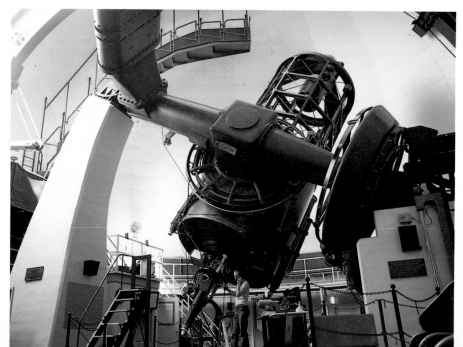

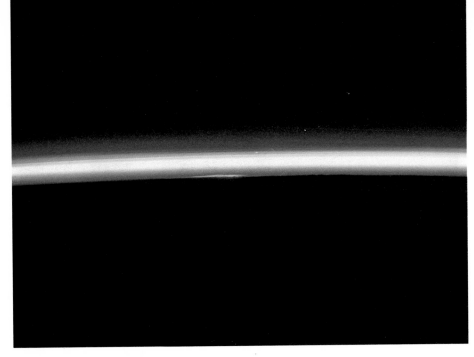

A sunset in outer space, photographed by astronaut Jeffrey Hoffman in 1985 from the 51-D Space Shuttle mission. The color bands show different layers of the atmosphere.

At some large observatories, scientists use *spectroscopes* to analyze the light that comes from objects in space. They are able to determine what chemical elements make up distant stars and to see if they are moving closer or farther away. Radiotelescopes gather radio waves given off by distant bodies. The largest radio telescope is at Arecibo, Puerto Rico. Its dish, a framework of perforated aluminum panels, is 305 m (1,000 ft) across.

Precision mirrors and the choice of location for observatories are critical to telescope technology. The best locations are in areas away from the glare of city lights, with high elevations and minimal air pollution. These features lessen the effects of atmospheric distortion and improve viewing capabilities.

After years of study and observation, scientists have put together a composite picture of the way the successive layers of Earth's atmosphere blend imperceptibly into space about 160 km (100 mi) above the Earth's surface. Deep space refers to regions from 190 km (120 mi) above the Earth to as far as the region of the Moon. Outer space usually means beyond the interplanetary regions. But as far as anyone knows, space is limitless.

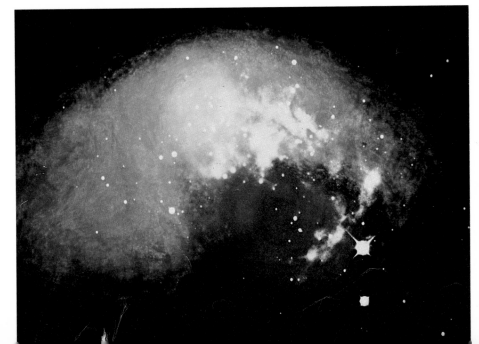

A 1982 map of the Orion Nebula taken through a telescope sensitive to infrared light.

GETTING THERE

By observation, calculation and speculation, scientists had pieced together a comprehensive though incomplete picture of the Universe by the early part of this century. But earthbound observation has its obvious limitations. Scientists realized that the only way to get to know space firsthand would be to go there.

Before spacecraft could be launched, scientists and engineers had to develop rockets with enormous force to overcome Earth's gravity. To go into orbital velocity, an object must be accelerated to 28,000 kph (16,800 mph). Once in orbit, that object can continue for a very long time since there is no air to slow it down.

One of the pioneers in rocketry was the Russian K.E. Tsiolkovsky (1857–1935). He was one of the first to understand what was needed to launch a vehicle into space. He also realized that if rockets were mounted one on top of another, the last, or top, one (and therefore the smallest and lightest one) would eventually travel the farthest. Although Tsiolkovsky was largely ridiculed in his own time, he is recognized today as a pioneer in space travel.

Today's space exploration would be far less advanced if it hadn't been for the early work of Robert Goddard (1882–1945). Fascinated by the possibilities of space travel, he built and experimented with rockets during much of the 1920s and later. In 1926 he launched the first liquid-propelled rocket. It flew a distance of 56 m (185 ft) and made Goddard the "father" of every rocket launch that has taken place since.

Another space pioneer was the German scientist Hermann Oberth (1894-   ). Germany was interested in rockets mainly for military purposes. By the late 1930s the Germans were preparing for war and they wanted to know more about rockets and their possibilities. Oberth's writings and experiments greatly influenced another of the key figures in twentieth century rocket building, Wernher von Braun (1912–1977).

Although Tsiolkovsky, Goddard and Oberth all had helped in the development of the modern rocket, it was Wernher von Braun, at the center of Hitler's war effort, who would leave the greatest

Two of the most influential space scientists: (left) the Russian Tsiolkovsky; (below) the German-born Wernher von Braun, who joined America's space program after World War II.

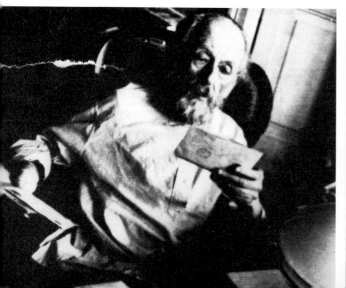

stamp on space travel. His great invention, the V-2 rocket, was not intended for outer space. It was originally designed to be launched from a site in Germany and sent across the English Channel to England to wreak death and destruction on the British population. In fact, the weapon came too late. Although it was tested as early as 1942, it was not operational until 1944, by which time the war was close to being lost by the Germans.

When World War II ended in 1945, von Braun surrendered, and was captured by the U.S. Army. His value as a scientist was recognized and he immediately became part of what was rapidly becoming a new and important project for the United States: the conquest of space. Several German V-2 rockets that von Braun had helped to develop were studied and tested by the United States in the late forties. After his surrender to the Allies in 1945, von Braun said that if the Germans had had the industrial power to mass produce V-2 rockets, they might have won the war. At the same time, other German rocket specialists went to work for the Soviet Union. Thus began the Space Race.

Today the Space Race is carried on by teams of scientists employed by huge government agencies. Some researchers work for universities or in private industry. The National Aeronautics and Space Administration (NASA) is responsible for the U.S. space program. A similar agency in the U.S.S.R. oversees that country's space exploration efforts. More recently fifteen nations have banded together to form the European Space Agency (ESA). Japan, too, is a contender in space and has its own space agency. Such concentrated efforts are needed to run the hugely expensive space launches and to operate space centers around the world.

THE U.S.S.R. DOES IT FIRST

On October 4, 1957 a new era in exploration began. A small, cylindrical sphere named Sputnik 1 changed world history. It was the world's first manmade satellite. Any body that revolves around another is a satellite. For instance, the Moon is a satellite of Earth and the Earth is a satellite of the Sun. Suddenly the world was faced with a new phenomenon—artificial satellites—instruments sent into orbit to relay information back to Earth.

Sputnik 1 circled the Earth about every 90 minutes in an oval orbit that ranged from 240 km (150 mi) to almost 960 km (600 mi) above the Earth's surface. The world's first artificial satellite weighed just 84 kg (185 lb) and its payload was little more than a thermometer hooked up to a battery-powered radio transmitter. Although the satellite was unmanned, radio transmitters were able to send information back to Earth. Because the Russians had wanted to be first in space, they shrouded everything surrounding the Sputnik program in absolute secrecy. No one was sure whether their satellites were for research or for defense.

A month later, while Sputnik 1 was still orbiting, the Soviets launched a second satellite. Sputnik 2, somewhat larger, carried the first living creature to be sent into outer space—a small dog named Little Curly. The dog came to be known throughout the world as Laika, the name of the breed. Her flight was the first attempt to discover how space affects living things. There wasn't enough oxygen for Laika, so the pup died. But on a later Sputnik flight in 1960, the dogs Strelka and Belka became the first animals retrieved alive from orbit. These experiments taught scientists much that they needed to know to keep humans alive and safe in outer space after launching.

To place a satellite into orbit requires vertical projection to the right altitude and then horizontal thrust to move it into a path parallel to the Earth's surface. Once the satellite is in orbit, solar cells supply power from solar energy and batteries then store that power.

Models of the first two Soviet satellites: (below left), **Sputnik 1 and** (below), **Sputnik 2.**

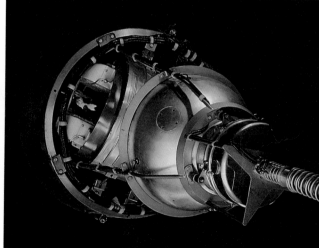

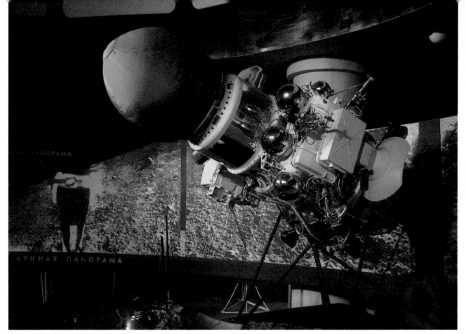

Satellites are almost always equipped with cameras to take pictures and radios to transmit data and receive commands by means of antennae directed towards precise points on Earth. Computers control the orientation of receptors and transmitters during orbit. Radiometers measure radiation. Repeating satellites have a radio transponder that receives, amplifies and retransmits messages.

After the Russians had tried satellites, they sought new ways to explore outer space. Space probes, unmanned spacecraft that carry instruments, have been one of the most effective ways to teach us about conditions in outer space. The earliest series of probes was targeted to reach the Moon. The Soviet Union's Luna probes began an era of direct investigation of other celestial bodies.

On the second day of 1959 the Soviets sent their Luna 1 to the Moon. But it wasn't until September of that year that a craft, Luna 2, actually reached the Moon. These Luna spacecraft sent back photos and information about the Moon. Luna 9 landed on the Moon in February 1966. Luna 10 became the first artificial satellite of the Moon and sent pictures from its dark side. These probes also gave detailed information about the solid, lava-like rock of the Moon's crust.

Left. **The more sophisticated Luna 17 Moon rover.** Below. **One of the world's best-known animals: the first creature in space, Laika.**

THE U.S. ENTERS THE RACE

The American space program got off the ground about two months after the Soviet Sputnik launch. In January 1958, the first U.S. satellite, Explorer I, blasted off attached to a rocket designed by Wernher von Braun. In December 1957, an earlier attempt had exploded soon after leaving the launch pad.

The U.S. rocket was smaller than the one used by Russia, but it made up in sophistication what it lacked in size. Explorer I was a 14-kg (31-lb) cylinder, just 15 cm (6 in) in diameter and 85 cm (34 in) long. Its instruments were the first to detect the bands of electromagnetic radiation that surround the Earth—the portion of the upper atmosphere now called the Van Allen belt.

Communications satellites were some of the earliest satellites put into orbit. In the 1960s, the Echo satellites were designed to relay radio signals. Another early U.S. satellite, TIROS I, launched in 1960, was one of the first to photograph weather patterns from outer space.

The Explorer series of launches was followed by the Vanguard lift-offs. Beginning in 1958, the United States launched the Pioneer series of space probes. The first Pioneer launches were trial-and-error efforts. Pioneer 5 was aimed towards Venus, but went into orbit around the Sun. It transmitted information for more than three months in 1960. Pioneer 6 sent data from deep space and Pioneer 7 worked as a solar weather satellite.

The Ranger program of the sixties was intended to send unmanned spacecraft to the Moon. The Ranger satellites—1 through 9—were powered by panels of solar cells. They sent back television pictures from the surface of the Moon. The Ranger probes were the first to be controlled by computer and sequencer modules that told the craft what to do and when to do it.

The Surveyor program was intended to place instrumentation modules, including photographic equipment and television cameras on the Moon's surface. The Surveyors were designed to "soft land." A soft landing is achieved by using a retrorocket to prevent the craft from crashing into the surface.

A Jupiter C rocket waits to launch the first U.S. satellite, Explorer 1, in 1958.

A 1968 photo of an Apollo 8 crew in training prior to actual spaceflight. They were being taught how to bail out in the water in case of an emergency. The picture gives some sense of the cramped quarters inside the craft.

The American lunar orbiters took pictures that were stored in the spacecraft and relayed back when the satellite passed the side of the Moon that faces Earth. Lunar Orbiter 1, launched in August 1966, maintained two-way radio contact with the Earth for more than ten days as it looked for a site for future Apollo landings.

Both Soviet and American space probes explored the planets during the 1960s and 1970s. The Mariner series were flyby planetary probes. Mariner 1 was launched towards Venus in July 1962, but had to be destroyed when it wandered from its course. Mariner 2 passed as close as 33,600 km (21,000 mi) to Venus and transmitted valuable information back to Earth. Mariner 3 failed but Mariner 4 was a successful flyby mission to Mars. Mariner 5 passed within 4,000 km (2,500 mi) of Venus in October 1967. The same month, a Soviet spacecraft, Venera 4, landed on the planet's surface. Both countries compared data confirming ultra-high temperatures and high atmospheric pressure underneath Venus's dense cloud cover. The planet's atmosphere may be as much as 95 percent carbon dioxide, and it is unlikely that anything could live there.

Early photographs of space: (above left) **a picture of the Milky Way galaxy. The diagonal line is the Echo 1 communications satellite's trail;** (above) **the Earth seen from a photo taken on a Gemini 7 mission.**

A model of one of the Surveyors that made five soft landings on the Moon between 1966 and 1968. This one was equipped with a special extendable claw for digging into the Moon's crust.

11

FIRST MANNED FLIGHTS

The first attempts at space travel had involved only machines and animals. As soon as people started going into space, interest shifted towards the personalities and achievements of the heroic men and women who flew in them. If people were to go into space, spacecraft had to be safe, and the design, shape and construction material of the vehicles became important.

On April 12, 1961 the Soviet cosmonaut Yuri A. Gagarin became the first human being to go into space. The Soviets call the people in their space program cosmonauts, which means ''sailors of the universe.'' Gagarin's Vostok 1 spacecraft flew around the Earth only once in a voyage that lasted only an hour and forty-eight minutes. The actual orbit time was eighty-eight minutes.

In the United States, Project Mercury surorbital flights were the first programs for manned space travel. On January 31, 1961, a chimpanzee named Ham made a flight. On May 5, 1961, Alan Shepard became the first American in space when his Mercury capsule, the Freedom 7, was launched with a Redstone 3 rocket from Cape Canaveral, Florida, on a flight that described a big arc. The flight lasted fifteen minutes and covered only 480 km (302 mi).

Less than a year later, Marine Colonel John H. Glenn became the first American astronaut to orbit the Earth. On February 20, 1962, Glenn climbed aboard a Mercury 6 spacecraft known as Friendship 7 and orbited the Earth three times, taking about five hours.

Meanwhile Vostok 2, with Gherman Titov in command, was launched by the Soviets in August 1961. It stayed aloft nearly twenty-five hours and circled the Earth seventeen times at a height of about 176 km (110 mi).

On March 18, 1965, Alekei Leonov left his Voskhod 2 capsule and became the first person to ''walk'' in space. The word ''float'' is closer to describing what Leonov actually did when he ventured outside his capsule into the weightless environment of space. Both Leonov and the American astronaut Edward White, who ten weeks later ''walked'' in space were tethered by a long nylon cord. White wore a specially designed space suit and helmet and carried a Self-Maneuvering Unit (SMU) that allowed him to move around.

Two of the best-known early space travelers: (below left) **Yuri Gagarin and** (below) **John Glenn.**

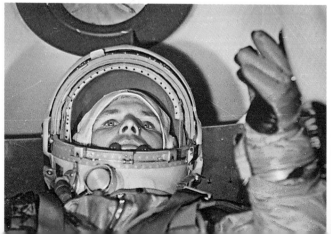

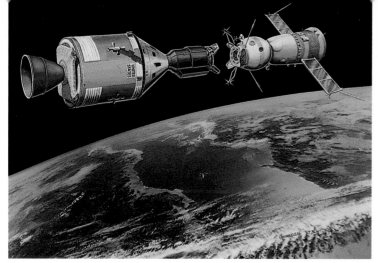

At first only one astronaut was sent aloft at a time, but soon flights carried crews of two, three or more people on board. Project Gemini followed the Mercury program. Its objectives were to test operations essential for the Moon program. John Young and Virgil Grissom made the first Gemini flight on March 23, 1965. They made three orbits and used orbit control rockets.

Gemini 6 and 7 made the first rendezvous in space on December 15, 1965. The spacecraft came within 3 m (10 ft) of each other and then orbited in tandem for four hours, finishing two nearly complete orbits. Then they separated and Gemini 6 returned to Earth on December 16 with Gemini 7 following two days later. Gemini 7 had stayed in space longest and had covered more than 9 km (5.7 mi).

The first orbital docking took place in 1966 when a Gemini 8 spacecraft linked up with an Agena target rocket. But a greater "first" came in 1975 when the United States Apollo and the Soviet Soyuz spacecraft met and linked up in space. It was a moment the world had waited for: two international crews meeting in space. The flight commanders first shook hands through a hatch. Then the astronauts and cosmonauts visited each other's spacecraft and signed a register while the craft were docked in orbit for two days, July 17 and 18, 1975.

Above left. **An artist's interpretation of the Apollo-Soyuz linkup.** Above. **Stafford and Leonov in the hatchway between the two spacecraft.**

Left. **Ed White's historic 1965 "space walk." Tethered to his Gemini 4 spacecraft, he remained outside for twenty-one minutes, becoming the first American to leave a spacecraft while it was in orbit.** Below. **The docked Apollo 9 Command and Service modules, with Earth in the background. David Scott is performing an extravehicular activity (EVA).**

MEN ON THE MOON

The Moon is about 400,000 km (240,000 mi) from Earth. But in July 1969 it was only as far away as the nearest television set. Millions of viewers the world over watched as one of the most important events of the twentieth century occurred at Tranquillity Base on July 21, 1969 (GMT). Two astronauts, Neil Armstrong and his colleague, Edwin "Buzz" Aldrin, made history by being the first people to step onto the surface of the Moon. The world listened intently as Armstrong spoke the words "That's one small step for a man, one giant leap for mankind." And now centuries-long speculation about the Moon was over. At long last, people had actually visited the Moon's surface.

On July 16, 1969, at 9:32 a.m. EDT the Saturn 5 rocket blasted off. In less than a minute it was going faster than the speed of sound. Eleven minutes and forty-two seconds after lift-off, the third stage of the Saturn 5 rocket was shut down and the astronauts of the Apollo 11 mission began to orbit the Earth. Less than three hours later a brief rocket blast directed them towards the Moon. Later, when the craft was closer to the Moon, another 6-minute firing brought the Apollo into the Moon's orbit. Further flight adjustments were made by a series of short rocket blasts.

Sunday July 20 began with breakfast and the "suiting up" of astronauts Armstrong and Aldrin. They then squeezed themselves into the lunar module, which separated from the command ship at 1:47 p.m. The lunar module *Eagle* then descended to the Moon's surface. Once there, Armstrong spent approximately two hours and twenty minutes exploring while Aldrin spent two hours. About 96 km

Below left. **Edwin Aldrin descends the steps of the Lunar Module ladder as he prepares to walk on the Moon.** Below. **Aldrin on the Moon's surface near a leg of the Module. Neil Armstrong took the photo. Footprints of the two astronauts are visible in the foreground.**

(60 mi) overhead Michael Collins piloted the Columbia command module, which remained in orbit around the Moon. A little more than eight days after the beginning of the flight the three astronauts were recovered after their splashdown in the Pacific.

The astronauts brought back over 22 kg (48 lb) of moon rocks for future laboratory study. Armstrong and Aldrin took many photographs of the historical event during their "stopover." They left behind a plaque inscribed: "We came in peace for all mankind." The astronauts also left behind various tools, including scientific instruments to measure geological movement under the Moon's crust and atomic particles from the Sun. After just four hours on the Moon's surface, the men returned to their landing module and blasted off. They linked up again with the command ship *Columbia* and returned to Earth.

The United States launched five further Apollo missions to the Moon. Between July 1969 and December 1972, twelve astronauts landed there. They spent a total of 180 man-hours working on the Moon's surface. The last manned lunar flight to date, Apollo 17, was launched on December 7, 1972. It was one of the most successful. On all of these missions one primary goal was the photographic mapping of different parts of the Moon's surface and the study of samples of rocks and debris. During the course of these missions, some 400 kg (850 lb) of rock samples were brought back. By studying the rocks, scientists have learned much new information about the makeup of the Moon and about its origins and development. We know now, for example, that solid rocks date the Moon's existence back over four billion years! Some scientists believe that the Moon was made when a huge chunk equal to about one-sixth the mass of the newly formed planet Earth was torn away and hurled into space, leaving a great gap in the side of our planet that became the basin of the Pacific Ocean.

THE WORLD OF ASTRONAUTS

When the Soviet cosmonaut Yuri Gagarin, in 1961 became the first person to travel into space, his feat was all the more remarkable because he had entered an alien environment and had survived to tell about it. His accomplishment was the first of many achievements to come over the next decades. Today Soviet cosmonauts are trained at a secret facility north of Moscow called Star City.

Astronaut activities would not be possible without the development of space suits. One of the greatest modern examples of problem solving, space suits are designed to make a hostile atmosphere safe and friendly to humans. Space suits are pressurized and air conditioned. Scientists have vastly improved space suits over the years, so that they are now sophisticated, almost comfortable uniforms for work in outer space.

The work of space exploration has spawned whole new scientific fields. Astronauts are trained in astrogeology, the study and analysis of meteorites, cosmic dust and rocks originating in space. Exobiology is the study of life outside the Earth. The work astronauts perform has led to advances in astronomy, biology, chemistry, physics and other fields, including space medicine.

Astronauts and cosmonauts are rigorously trained for their work. Long sessions in simulators—machines that reproduce the conditions of their spacecraft—expose them to almost every possible danger and condition. Safety and equipment maintenance are emphasized. Strangely, the first human fatalities in the U.S. space program occurred on the ground. On January 27, 1967, three Apollo astronauts—Grissom, White and Chaffee—died in a launch pad flash fire probably caused by an electrical malfunction.

Below left. **Cosmonaut Valentina Tereshkova inside a Vostok capsule, and** below, **her colleague Yuri Romanenko on board Soyuz.**

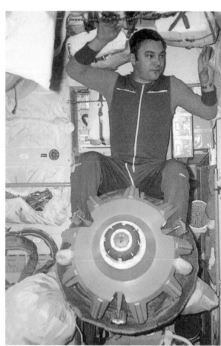

Weightlessness becomes familiar in a series of tests in a diving airplane. Many space tests are performed in flotation tanks or under water, where the weightless conditions of space can be approximated. The crew for the Space Shuttle spends time in a testing device called the WET-F, which stands for Weightless Environmental Training Facility.

The weightless environment of space affects just about any activity. Even eating and sleeping require special skills. Astronauts squeeze prepared food and beverages into their mouths from plastic wrappers. Astronaut food is mostly in powdered or dehydrated form and sealed in plastic sachets. Hot or cold water is added to the packet through a tube. The food is kneaded to form a paste that is then sucked through another tube. Astronauts have to be strapped down or zipped into sleeping bags to keep them from floating around the cabin while they sleep.

Above left. **Cosmonauts undergo training in a water tank that simulates the weightless conditions of space.** Above. **Astronauts on board a NASA aircraft undergo "weightless" training.**

Far left. **Astronaut Sally Ride on mid-deck of the *Challenger* during a 1983 mission. She was in constant communication with mission control on the ground.** Below. **Astronaut Guion Bluford is being checked out on a treadmill after a space flight.**

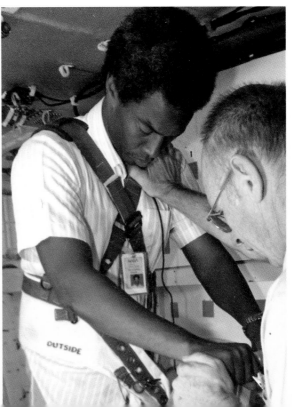

PICTURES FROM SPACE

One of the most important activities aboard a spacecraft is photography, and the vistas from space are matchless. Photos taken in space have a remarkable clarity because they are free of Earth's atmospheric distortion.

The early Surveyor lunar pictures were blurry and hard to read, but gave indications of what was to come. In the early 1970s, Skylab 3 took photos that showed solar eruptions. Mariner 10 took extensive pictures of Venus in 1974.

The manned Gemini 12 mission in November 1966 was significant for the number of photographs taken. Captain James Lovell and Major Edwin Aldrin took pictures of a total solar eclipse as well as ultraviolet images of stars.

In 1975 the United States launched two Viking space probes to search for life on Mars, the planet that scientists believe is most like Earth. Special landing probes touched down on the surface of the planet in 1975 and September 1976. Each probe was about the size of a compact car. The probes remained in place for several years and continued to send back data and photographs. Viking 2 showed a reddish surface much like that seen in pictures taken by Viking 1, although that landing had taken place more than 6,400 km (4,000 mi) away. Colors of the rock and soil were almost identical at the two landing sites. Scientists found some conditions that were favorable to life, but did not discover any evidence of even microscopic life forms. They concluded that the planet is too cold and dry to support life.

Landsat, launched by the United States in 1972, took thousands of photographs of the Earth's surface that have enabled scientists and researchers to assess long-term environmental problems. Satellite maps have made it possible to monitor Earth's ice caps, deserts, forests and waterways, and even plant distributions and the migrations of land and sea animals.

One of the earliest Landsat photos, taken in 1972, of the southern California coast. The picture shows the San Andreas fault, an area of high earthquake activity. The photo also identified several smaller faults that were previously unknown.

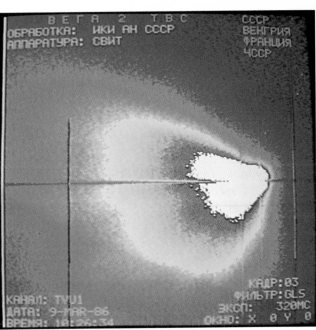

ВЕГА 2 ТВС
ОБРАБОТКА: ИКИ АН СССР
АППАРАТУРА: СВИТ
СССР
ВЕНГРИЯ
ФРАНЦИЯ
ЧССР
КАДР: 03
КАНАЛ: ТVU1 ФИЛЬТР: GLS
ДАТА: 9-MAR-86 ЭКСП: 320MC
ВРЕМЯ: 10:26:34 ОКНО: X 0 Y 0

Landsat was the first satellite designed specifically to monitor the Earth's natural resources. Landsat (once known as ERTS, for Earth Resources Technology Satellite) was followed by Landsat 2 in 1975. These satellites showed geological fault lines indicating earthquake activity. Filters recorded separate images in three colors—green, red and infrared. Then the images were reassembled in laboratories on the ground. Most space photos are color and computer enhanced to highlight particular features.

Unmanned American probes have visited every planet except Pluto. Venus seems to have an oppressive atmosphere and may be the hottest planet, with surface temperatures of up to 470°C (878°F).

Voyager 1 took photos of Jupiter in 1979 from a distance of 40 million km (25 million mi). Jupiter's satellite, Ganymede, showed up clearly in the pictures since it is larger than the planet Mercury! In 1981, Voyager 2 photographed Saturn and its rings from a distance of 21 million km (13 million mi). Uranus was filmed in 1986, and showed great clouds, indicating a smog-like atmosphere.

More recently, the Soviets' Vega 2 space probe was used to photograph the return of Halley's Comet in 1986. Today a Soviet agency is selling sharper pictures from space than its French and American counterparts.

Above left. **Saturn's rings are clearly seen in profile and in cross-section in this 1981 Voyager 2 photo.** Above. **A Vega 2 visualization of the 1986 return of Halley's Comet.**

Viking 2 photo of Mars shows dusty, arid terrain with no indication of supporting life.

A REUSABLE VEHICLE

As World War II drew to a close, Wernher von Braun and his colleagues in Nazi Germany were already working on a new generation of advanced rockets that would travel in pairs. The smaller (A-9) module would then return to the ground. This idea for a returnable, reusable, rocket-propelled spacecraft was the first step towards the U.S. Space Shuttle program.

Before the Shuttle, satellites were launched into space by three-stage rockets that could be used only once. The *Columbia*, the first Space Shuttle, differed from earlier rocket launchers in that its orbiter could be used again and again. The Shuttle is built of high-strength aluminum alloys and silica insulating tiles to protect against overheating. At 32.2 m (122 ft) long and with a wingspan of 23.8 m (78 ft), the orbiter resembles an ordinary plane.

Fully fueled, the Space Shuttle weights 2.2 million kg (4.5 million lb) at liftoff. The orbiter itself, when returning, weighs only about 84,000 kg (185,000 lb). The payload bay is 4.5 m (15 ft) wide by 18.2 m (60 ft) long. The rocket boosters are the heaviest parts of the Shuttle. The booster gives the initial liftoff; when its fuel is used up, the booster drops off. The second stage lifts another rocket higher until it too is used up and drops off. The third, and final, stage carries the Shuttle into orbit.

Space rockets burn either solid or liquid propellants. All rocket propellants must include a supply of oxygen since there is none in space to support combustion. The Space Shuttle uses a solid propellant mixed with synthetic rubber.

Soon after the Space Shuttle made its first voyage on April 12, 1981, it became the most popular feature of the U.S. space program since the first Moon landing and Shuttle astronauts were popular heros.

A view of Spacelab aboard the Space Shuttle.

Below left. **A photo of Skylab 4 taken by Gerald Carr standing above the Apollo Telescope Mount.** Below. **A view of Skylab in orbit. There should have been a matching "wing" on the opposite side of the capsule.**

Just a few meters away from the Space Shuttle, Bruce McCandless uses his nitrogen-propelled Manned Maneuvering Unit (MMU) to move around outside the Shuttle.

With a fixed camera on his space suit helmet, McCandless took this 1984 photo of the *Challenger*. The cargo bay is clearly visible.

From the beginning, the Space Shuttle's cargo, called payload, attracted a lot of attention. Among the most useful payloads has been Spacelab, an orbiting laboratory. The ESA built the lab for work by an international team of scientists. It is a long, tunnel-like "room" attached to the orbiter by another, smaller tunnel.

After a ten-year development period, Spacelab finally flew on *Columbia* on November 28, 1983. The Spacelab crew took many photos of the Earth's surface and conducted experiments. A later laboratory structure, the Long Duration Exposure Facility (LDEF), containing instrumentation drawers that hold experiments, went up in 1984.

In 1973–74, Skylab, an experimental space station and a forerunner of Spacelab, was sent into orbit. Skylab was 36.5 m (120 ft) long and weighed 90,700 kg (200,000 lb). After it was launched in May 1973, Skylab remained aloft for about 6 months. During this time three different crews of three astronauts each worked in the lab a total of 171 days. To make the project completely international, scientists were recruited from some eighteen countries.

The first crew got an unexpected job when one of Skylab's two solar panels disappeared. Designed to protect the lab from the Sun's brutal heat, the panels needed to be repaired. The first job was to reposition Skylab from the ground and the second was to send the astronauts outside to erect parasol-like sun shields.

Scientists aboard Skylab performed medical, scientific and technological experiments. These included seeing if spiders would spin webs in weightless conditions. The success of Skylab was final proof that humans could endure the conditions of outer space for long periods of time and remain healthy.

THE CHALLENGER AND AFTER

Just when Space Shuttle flights were beginning to seem almost routine, tragedy struck. On the frigid morning of January 28, 1986 seven astronauts—including the first schoolteacher to go into space—were only seventy-three seconds into the flight when the orbiter and its fuel tanks exploded in a ball of fire. As spectators on the ground watched in horror, the spacecraft split apart and fell back to Earth in fragments that were scattered over many miles. The entire world was shocked and the U.S. space program was shut down for more than two and a half years.

The wreckage of the *Challenger* was recovered with the assistance of manned and unmanned submersibles which combed the Atlantic Ocean off the coast of Cape Canaveral. Months of investigation traced the malfunction to a defective solid-fuel rocket booster. Some experts feel that solid-fuel rockets are dangerous because, once ignited, they cannot be turned off.

On that fateful journey, the Space Shuttle's crew included two women for the first time. One was the veteran astronaut Judith Resnick, but the other was an elementary schoolteacher from a small New England town. Christa McAuliffe had been specially recruited and trained to fly aboard the Shuttle and teach a class lesson from space to children in the United States and around the world. But the *Challenger* disaster taught another kind of lesson to the world: to proceed with caution when venturing into new territory.

While the U.S. Space Shuttle program was shut down, the Soviets took the lead in manned space flight, in launch rate and in heavy lift-off launchers. In September 1988 a Soviet and an Afghan cosmonaut in a Soyuz TM-5 capsule left the Mir space station to return to Earth only to experience trouble with their computerized navigation system. Apparently infrared sensors malfunctioned. After two unsuccessful re-entry attempts and with food and oxygen supplies running out, the two managed to land their spacecraft safely in Soviet Central Asia.

Christa McAuliffe, a schoolteacher from New England, was the first civilian to fly on a Space Shuttle mission.

The *Challenger* lifts off on January 28, 1986. Seconds later, tragedy struck.

On the ground in Houston, Texas, mission controllers couldn't grasp what was being shown on their TV monitors.

Refinements in design have taken place to ensure that the *Challenger* accident can never happen again. The *Discovery* astronauts underwent rigorous testing while the Shuttle program was on hold. In simulated situations, astronauts are being trained to handle every conceivable type of malfunction including escape from an aborted flight.

Proposed improvements to the Space Shuttle program include expansion of NASA's fleet of orbiters to five, to allow for additional backup and emergency coverage. There is also a plan to change the orbiter design to increase its maximum flight capability from ten to fourteen days. Longer flights will require added oxygen capacity. Is manned space flight worth all the risks? This is a question that the *Challenger* accident raised over and over again. Almost half of Americans asked feel that too much money is being spent on developing the space program. For obvious financial reasons, it may make sense to link up with the USSR or other international space agencies to finance expensive missions, such as future trips to Venus and Mars.

The completion in October 1988 of the successful flight of the new Space Shuttle *Discovery* meant that the American space program was back on track. More than 400 design improvements made the *Discovery* a better, safer space vehicle. The Soviets seized the opportunity to launch their own version of the Shuttle just a month later. Interestingly, the Soviet shuttle is almost identical to the U.S. prototype.

As a result of the *Challenger* tragedy, astronauts are now trained for emergency evacuation.

On October 3, 1988 the *Discovery* touched down in California, symbolizing the return of the U.S. Space Shuttle program.

SPACE UPDATE

In October 1987 Soviet scientists marked the thirtieth anniversary of Sputnik by hosting a conference of about four-thousand space scientists, educators, astronauts, and space agency officials from around the world. One of the items discussed was the progress in satellite design over those thirty years. The first Sputnik was very basic: a small metal globe sent into orbit over the Earth.

Now, more than thirty years later, nearly all the spacecraft that have been launched have become satellites of Earth and more than 5,000 satellites have been sent into orbit. Today's satellites are far more than big tin cans floating in space. They are equipped with a variety of instruments, cameras, tape recorders and radio transmitters to report the readings of these instruments. On some satellites, special sensors detect and measure radiation.

Of many shapes and sizes, satellites have caused a revolution in our knowledge of astronomy, weather forecasting and communications. The ESA's communications satellite, EUTELSAT, was first put into orbit by the ESA in the 1970s. This relays telephone calls and television signals all over the world. Today a global network of satellites handles television program transmittal, telephone calls and telex messages.

Most nations and the ESA have relied on satellites placed in low polar orbits. This means that the satellite passes over both the North and South poles in its orbit around the Earth. In 1983, the Infrared Astronomical Satellite (IRAS) was launched by the Netherlands, Great Britain and the United States. IRAS was designed to detect infrared radiation coming from space and to record its effects.

Satellites for international defense are among the most controversial—and secret—space projects. The U.S. Strategic Defense Initiative (SDI, but commonly called "Star Wars") is designed to protect the United States from a nuclear attack by another power. It will consist of a network of satellites, orbiting at various levels, that can detect and intercept enemy rockets launched anywhere on Earth. Many people feel it is a waste of money and resources; others think the concept is too complex to be effective. Still others see it as a possible end to war.

The Soviet Energia rocket on its launching pad.

The Soviet Space Station Mir being assembled on the ground below **and** left **in flight in 1986.**

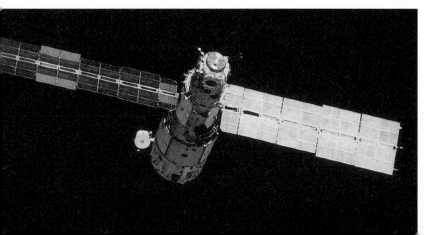

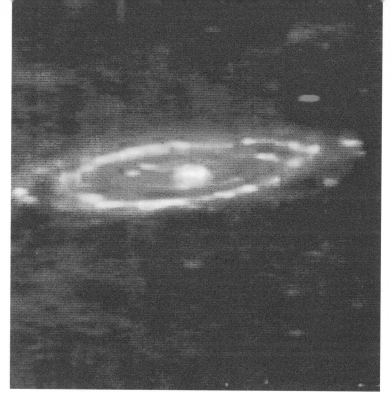

At the Soviet space station Mir (a Russian word meaning "peace"), cosmonaut Yuri Romanenko set a record in 1987 by remaining in space for 326 days. The flight tested a human's ability to withstand the prolonged time in space required for interplanetary travel. The Soviet Mir is the latest version of the Salyut space stations that were developed in the 1970s.

Although Mir is not enormous—it is half the size of the U.S. Skylab—its 17-m (56-ft) length can be extended. Mir has been permanently staffed since February 1987. To the best of anyone's knowledge, the Soviet space stations are intended to mix scientific with military and commercial research.

In 1987 the United States launched eight rockets; the U.S.S.R. launched 95. Once again, the Soviets have the lead in space, just as they did in 1957, when it all began. The Soviet Union has launched steadily and often; the result is a broad base of space programs. By early 1988 the Soviets had logged 5,000 days of manned space travel compared to the American 1,800.

The Soviet Energia, the world's most powerful rocket to date, is entirely reusable and is designed for use with the Soviet Space Shuttle. This is a major breakthrough. The rocket can boost payloads of around 200 tons into space. This is more than three times the capacity of the Space Shuttle. The rocket can also be recovered for reuse. It is designed in seven parts, each of which falls gently back to earth by parachute when the fuel in its liquid fuel compartment is spent. Energia is similar to the U.S. Saturn 5 rockets that carried astronauts to the Moon and back. But work on the Saturn program was discontinued when the Space Shuttle program was approved.

Ariane 4, the new commercial "workhorse" for ESA, was introduced in 1988. It faces strong competition from the Soviet Union and China, but its launch site near the Equator makes it more fuel efficient. In a few years Japan may have a similar launcher available for use.

THE CURRENT SPACE AGENDA

Several things are at stake in the Soviets' apparent lead in the Space Race. Whoever gets a permanent station in space first then takes that lead; this leadership will become one of the key factors in the years ahead. The Russians are aware of the commercial value of space; with this recognition and *glasnost* (the policy of "openness") has come a more cooperative attitude.

NASA's immediate agenda calls for the resumption of the Space Shuttle program, with thirty more flights due by the end of 1992. Most of these missions will carry research satellites into space for launching, including the Magellan satellite to Venus, the Galileo probe to Jupiter and the Hubble Space Telescope. In the 1990s work will begin on a space station and the Shuttle will ferry people and materials to the site.

NASA's space station will be built in two steps. First a large structural beam will be built to serve as a central framework to which modules can be anchored. The second phase requires the construction of two perpendicular beams to anchor additional modules and power panels as well as a separate orbiting platform for space vehicle docking. All of this is extremely expensive, and by the time it is built, the space station could cost well over $50 billion.

The station will be approximately 105 m (345 ft) tall and 155 m (500 ft) across and will orbit about 480 km (300 mi) above the Earth. The modules will be provided by NASA and other international space agencies. The ESA and Japan will provide experiment modules, and Canada will contribute remote manipulator arms. An array of solar panels will provide electrical power.

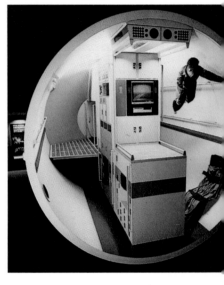

A model showing conditions at a space station. Sections called modules could be added or removed as needed. Some would hold labs and some would provide living space.

An artist's interpretation of the Hubble Space Telescope.

It has become more and more evident to scientists and researchers that Earth-based telescopes are very limited. It is necessary to go farther out into space for the best results. Orbiting satellites have made space telescopes possible. Earth's atmosphere absorbs and distorts light rays as well as X-rays, ultraviolet and gamma rays. But orbiting astronomical satellites are able to receive these rays and relay data back to Earth.

NASA's Hubble Space Telescope has been ready since January 1986. Now set to be launched in 1989, it will be deployed from the Space Shuttle with the remote manipulating system (RMS) robot arm. The telescope measures over 13 m (43 ft) long and weighs nearly 11 tons. Powered by solar devices, its reflector is 2.4 m (8 ft) in diameter. It will orbit Earth at a height of 500 km (300 mi) and be able to detect objects invisible even to much stronger telescopes on Earth. The Hubble Space Telescope is the keystone of a planned network of four orbiting observatories that will cover the range of cosmic radiation.

The current NASA slate calls for a Mars probe in 1992, an atmospheric probe to Saturn a few years later, a possible mission to Mars's moon Phobos by 2000 and building an observatory on the Moon's dark side by 2004. Plans are also on the drawing board for a space plane that will take off from and land on a runway—without a rocket launch. It will travel at twenty-five times the speed of sound.

The Soviet Union plans to use the Energia rocket to send a massive unmanned mission to Mars in 1992, the first of six probes planned over the next decade. Soviet scientists hope to have a manned mission on Mars by 2000. To this end they have already performed thousands of experiments in *Kvant,* their orbiting laboratory.

As the costs involved in maintaining a space program escalate, international cooperation becomes more and more important. Fourteen nations participated in the Soviet's Vega mission to Halley's Comet. The years ahead will see even more extensive sharing of technology and resources.

THE FUTURE OF SPACE

Space is the true new frontier, and some people think there should be no dividing line between Earth and space. The general feeling is that, despite dangers and high costs, we need to continue to explore. The challenge must be met.

In the twenty-first century, astronauts will almost certainly travel to Mars. Mars presents the possibility of human colonies because it seems to most resemble the environment of Earth. Since Mars and Earth reach the closest points in their orbits every two and one half years, 2003, 2005 or 2008 have been proposed as dates for the first Mars mission, because these are the years when such planetary "conjunctions" will occur.

The Mariner and Viking probes provided many dazzling photographs of the Martian world—its mountains, volcanoes and ice caps—but there have been, to date, no signs of living things. Before manned trips to Mars are attempted, more unmanned probes will be needed. Scientists will need to know for sure if there are any potentially harmful microorganisms in the Martian soil.

Engineers are currently at work designing robots that can explore space or build colonies there. There are many places where it is easier and safer to send a machine than a person. Robots do not get tired and do not need air, food, water or light. Robots equipped with cameras, sensors and special computers can explore almost as well as humans. They would be ideal for longer missions in space, especially those that might take several years.

Our future in space exploration has been the subject of wild speculation. The next generation of scientists will have to consider the limits imposed by budgets and resources, technology and human physiology. But the colonization of space is a real possibility.

A possible space station configuration. Assembly and repair tasks will be done by astronauts, aided by robot arms and other mechanized equipment. This team will be able to add to the structure.

A lunar outpost possibility, showing space nuclear power units in the background.

Once the first space colonies are established, scientists expect the space population to double every twenty-five years. They say by the year 2050—about sixty years from now—one million people may live in space. Experts think we can expect a total space population of 1,000,000,000,000 by 2550!

How would all these people be kept alive? Space contains a wealth of resources—gases, metal and minerals. There is an almost limitless potential to develop raw materials for mills, refineries and factories. Vast greenhouses would be needed to grow the food to supply these space colonies.

One of the biggest questions scientists hope to answer is this: Does life exist in space? And, if so, what is it like? Meteorites demonstrate that organic compounds are formed in space. But if life exists in space, it remains to be found.

The time line of all space exploration spans an incredibly short part of the history of the world—just a little more than thirty years. Much has been accomplished in this short time, but a Universe remains to be explored.

A space colony orbiting between the Earth and Moon in the 21st century. The entire doughnut-shaped ring would spin slowly, providing artificial gravity for the space colonists living there.

DATELINES

1926. Goddard launches first liquid-propelled rocket.

1930. Clyde Tombaugh discovers Pluto, the last planet to be found.

1945. Wernher von Braun, German rocket expert, surrenders to the Allies and enters the U.S. space program.

October 4, 1957. Soviet Union launches the first satellite, Sputnik 1.

November 1957. Sputnik 2 carries the dog Laika into space.

January 31, 1958. The first successful U.S. satellite launch sends Explorer 1 into orbit.

January 31, 1961. The United States makes suborbital flight with Ham the Chimp on board.

April 12, 1961. Yuri Gagarin becomes the first human to go into space and orbit the Earth.

May 5, 1961. Alan Shepard becomes the first American to enter space on a suborbital flight.

February 20, 1962. John Glenn becomes the first American astronaut to orbit the Earth.

March 18, 1965. Aleksei Leonov makes the first space walk from Voshkod 2.

March 23, 1965. Astronauts Grissom and Young participate in the first U.S. Gemini flight.

1966. Surveyor 1 tests equipment designed for soft landing on the Moon.

January 27, 1967. Launchpad tragedy kills three astronauts: Grissom, White, Chaffee.

July 20, 1969. Apollo 8 mission lands on the Moon and Neil Armstrong becomes the first human to set foot on the Moon.

December 1972. Last of 6 Apollo missions to the Moon begins.

May 14, 1973. Skylab is launched, and on May 25, the crew repairs the damaged station.

July 17-18, 1975. U.S. Apollo and Soviet Soyuz spacecraft make history by linking up in space.

1975. Two U.S. Viking probes search for life on Mars.

1978. Pluto's moon Charon is discovered.

1979. Voyager 1 begins its probe of Jupiter.

April 12, 1981. The U.S. Space Shuttle makes its maiden flight.

November 28, 1983. Spacelab is launched in a Space Shuttle flight.

January 28, 1986. Space Shuttle *Challenger* explodes, killing all on board. U. S. space program put on hold.

1988. U.S. Space Shuttle program is restored with launch of *Discovery*.

1988. Soviets unveil their Space Shuttle program.

1990s. Soviets plan two unmanned missions to Mars by 1992.

1995. Projected date for first section of U.S. space station to be put in space.

2000. Soviet Union hopes to send manned mission to Mars.

GLOSSARY

ASTRONAUT The name given to an American space traveler.

ATMOSPHERE The body of gases surrounding a planet or other body in space.

BOOSTER The first stage of a rocket that gives enough thrust to clear the Earth's gravity.

CAPSULE The portion of a spacecraft in which people travel.

COSMONAUT The name given to a Soviet space traveler.

DEEP SPACE The area of space between the Earth's atmosphere and the Moon.

EXTRAVEHICULAR ACTIVITY (EVA) An activity that takes place outside a spacecraft and requires the use of a space suit.

EXTRAVEHICULAR MOBILITY UNIT (EMU) Part of a space suit that helps astronauts move around.

FLYBY A mission that "flies by" or near an object in space.

HEAT SHIELD Portion of a space capsule that absorbs heat during re-entry.

LAUNCH "WINDOW" The period of best conditions for a space launch.

LIFTOFF The stage when a rocket leaves the launchpad, usually provided by rocket thrust.

ORBIT The path in which a planet moves around the Sun, or a satellite travels around the Earth.

ORBITER The plane-shaped part of the U.S. Space Shuttle, and the part that returns to Earth.

PAYLOAD The cargo carried in a spacecraft, often instruments or experiments.

PROPELLANT Fuel used to send a rocket into space.

PROPULSION The "push" that sends a rocket into orbit.

RE-ENTRY The point at which a spacecraft re-enters the Earth's atmosphere.

RENDEZVOUS A meeting in space of two spacecraft.

RETROROCKET A small rocket that is used to maneuver a spacecraft.

SATELLITE An object (which can be natural or artificial) that orbits around another, larger body in space.

SIMULATOR A training facility that reproduces conditions of, for example, space.

SOFT LANDING A landing by a spacecraft that does not damage the equipment.

SOLAR SYSTEM The Sun, plus the planets and their satellites which revolve around the Sun.

SPACE PROBES Unmanned space missions designed to collect information.

SPACE RACE The race between the Soviet Union and the United States for supremacy in space.

SPACEWALK An extravehicular activity (EVA) by astronauts in space suits.

SPUTNIK The first Soviet satellite.

SUBORBITAL FLIGHT A space flight that makes only a portion of an orbit of the Earth.

THRUST The force that propels a rocket into space.

INDEX